Exposure Mastery: Aperture, Shutter Speed & ISO

• The Difference Between Good and
Breathtaking Photographs •

By Brian Black

Check Out My Other Best-Selling Book:

• <u>DSLR Photography for Beginners</u>

Table of Contents

Introduction: About Light

If you've bought an expensive, high-quality camera, you want to do more with it than just point and shoot. You've invested in a good camera because you want to get serious about photography, maybe explore it as a profession. Certainly you want to explore the possibilities in photography as an art form.

Photography as creative art flows from the physics of photography. It's all about light, just as vision itself is all about light.

Light reflects from objects, passes through and is focused by the lens, and strikes something that registers the light and creates a picture. In the eye, that something is the retina, which sends information to the brain via the optic nerve. In a conventional film camera, the light is focused on a chemically-treated plastic strip that undergoes chemical changes in response to light energy. In a digital camera, the working part is an electronic sensor that creates a packet of information, which the camera stores in digital memory.

But in each of these methods of creating a picture of the world, the key role is played by light – and in photography, light is measured as *exposure*. How long the camera's sensor is exposed to light (shutter speed), how much light is allowed in at once (aperture), and how sensitive the sensor is to light

(ISO) determine the quality of the image. Digital cameras come with light meters that automatically set these three variables to achieve a "good" photographic image, but the creative part of photography comes, in large measure, from bypassing that automatic snapshot setting and taking control of the exposure yourself.

There's a reciprocal relationship between aperture and shutter speed. The narrower the aperture, the less light is allowed into the camera at any moment. The faster the shutter speed, the less light is allowed in over the time of exposure. This means that if you need to allow more light in to take a picture in dim lighting, you can do this either by slowing down the shutter speed or by widening the aperture. Either approach will allow sufficient exposure, but produce a very different effect. A wide aperture creates low depth of field, with only a small area in focus and objects closer or more distant rendered out of focus. A narrow aperture creates high depth of field, with more of the picture in focus and not as much left as a blur. A fast shutter speed captures motion sharply and crisply, while a slow shutter speed shows traces of objects in motion as a streak across the image. Clearly, then, using a narrow aperture (with a slow shutter speed to compensate) produces a very different image than using a fast shutter speed (with a wider aperture to compensate). That's only one example of creative control of exposure.

In this book, we'll cover the technical details of exposure and how the triangle of ISO, aperture, and shutter speed operates. You'll find definitions for terms like f-stop, and explanations of the numerical values used to describe photography elements. More importantly, you'll find a lot of ideas about how to use exposure and all the factors affecting it to create desired effects in your photography. The goal is to let you move beyond point and shoot to become an artist with your camera.

Recommended Equipment

If you want to take advantage of the possibilities inherent in digital SLR photography, you're going to have to spend a bit of money on a good camera and accessories. However, there's still a pretty wide range of prices. As long as you go with a well-respected manufacturer, you can expect quality. That said, the biggest and best camera makers are Canon and Nikon, so if you're going to buy a DSLR camera, it's highly recommended that you get one made by either of the two.

Creative Digital Photography: The Parts

Your camera is a complicated machine, although in fact a digital camera reduces the complexity somewhat compared to a film camera. The camera body, the lens, the light sensor, the shutter, the light meter, and – what we'll be focusing on in this book – the exposure controls, all contribute to the quality of the images.

At least as important as the camera and accessories, however, is what you do with them. Photography isn't just a mechanical process (or an electronic one). It's an art, and as a visual art it requires a good eye, a sense of perspective and beauty, and an understanding of the way to create photographic images that show what you want them to show in the way that you want. The camera differs from your eye in important ways. Just because you see a particular image doesn't mean that it will show up in the picture as you see it just by pointing and clicking the shutter release.

It's important to understand the limits of what the camera sees and how to use those limits to your advantage.

What's Involved?

The elements of creative photography come down to four things: framing or picture composition, focus, exposure, and graphic image control. The first three of these go into taking the picture, while the last is done with the image file afterwards using graphic software.

Of the three picture-taking elements, composition, focus, and exposure, exposure is the most versatile and also the trickiest to master. While all of them are important and deserve a lot of attention, the range of effects that can be created by varying the factors impacting exposure are especially broad and allow much room for creativity. There are several elements to this.

First, you can deliberately underexpose or overexpose a picture for effects. The light meter tells you what exposure to use to produce the best quality picture given the amount of light that's available. Underexposing the image gives you a dark, shadowy picture. Overexposing it gives a washed out effect.

Second, you can vary the exposure triangle, while leaving the overall exposure at "optimum" (or along with deliberately over- or underexposing the image). This produces a wide variety of effects, from crystal-sharp panoramas to streaked images imparting a sense of motion, from tightly focused close-ups to detail-revealing stop-motion photography.

Each of the three points of the exposure triangle – shutter speed, aperture (or "f-stop") and ISO – produces its own range of effects.

The most important tool in photography is knowledge, but there are some mechanical tools that can help, too. Among these are a tripod, a remote shutter release, different lenses and filters.

Understanding Aperture

Aperture refers to the size of the opening in the camera body that lets light through. It's controlled by a mechanical device, not electronically: an iris opening much like the iris of your eye, which serves the exact same purpose.

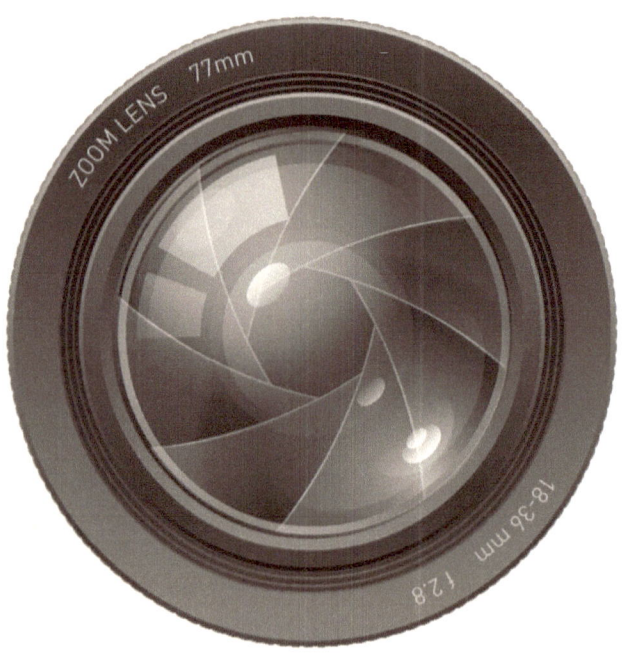

View of a camera's aperture from the front. Note the iris opening.

Aperture at its simplest is just a small hole for light to pass through, like a pinhole. (In fact, pinholes represent the simplest camera arrangements and pinhole cameras are still used in some applications.) When light passes through a small hole, it forms an inverted (that is, upside-down) image of the object it's reflected from on a surface opposite the hole. In a nutshell, that's how a camera works. The sensor in your camera "reads" this image and converts it into digital information, which is stored electronically in your camera's memory. From this storage, it can be transferred to a computer for processing using graphics software.

The variability of the aperture also allows you a range of effects involving *depth of field*.

What is Depth of Field?

Depth of field refers to how much of the picture is in focus, based on distance from the camera. The immediate object of focus of the picture will usually be in focus (unless you deliberately compose the picture to make it out of focus), but other objects further away or closer may or may not be. Whether they are or not is largely a function of the aperture: the size of the hole through which light passes.

Why? Because of the way light passes through the hole in the camera. When light goes through the hole cleanly, perpendicular to the light sensor at the rear of the camera, the result is a sharp, clear image. When light comes in at an angle, however, it becomes distorted and the image is fuzzy. A narrow aperture doesn't allow much light to enter the camera at an angle (it's completely blocked by the edges of the hole when it tries to do this), so most of the light that penetrates comes in perpendicular to the sensor and produces a sharp image. A wide aperture, on the other hand, allows light to enter the camera from a wider field and from more directions, so that more of the image is blurred.

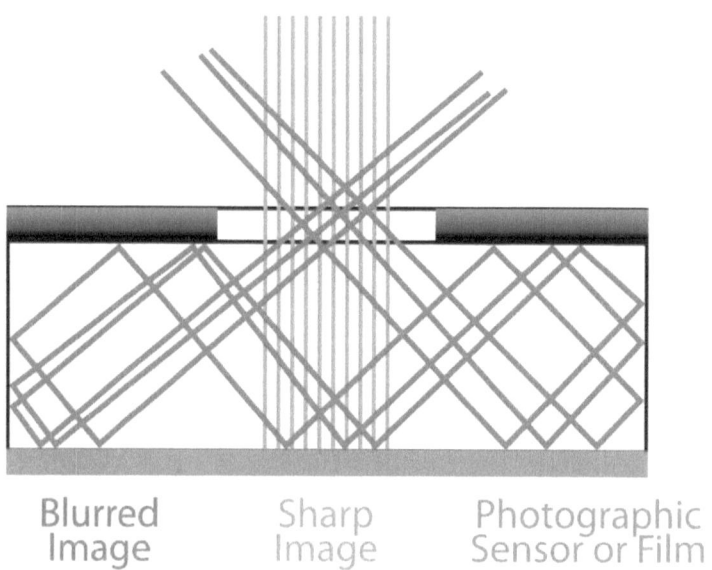

Blurred   Sharp   Photographic
Image   Image   Sensor or Film

Depth of field in photography is something like depth perception in vision, in that both involve the third dimension, depth. A photographic image is two dimensional. It has height and width, but no depth. But the scene being photographed is three dimensional. When you focus your camera lens on a particular object, say a face in a portrait, you ensure that this object will appear crisply and in focus in the final image (barring things like motion blur). With a high depth of field, you will also see objects behind the focus crisply. With a narrow depth of field, the object of focus will be surrounded by a soft blur.

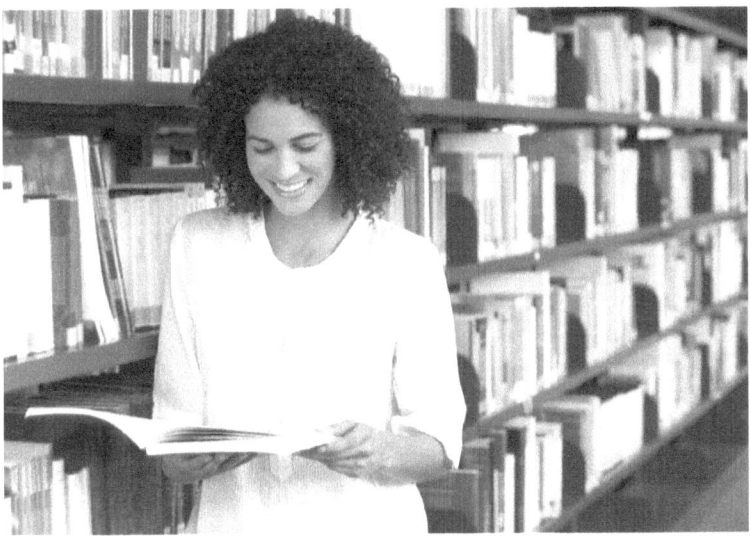

In this photo, note that the woman is in sharp focus, while the book stacks behind her are out of focus. This is an example of low depth of field.

As a general rule, low depth of field is good for portraits, close-up photography, and other situations where only a single object is important in the picture and the rest of it is background. You actually don't want crisp focus for all objects in such a photograph. It would make the picture too cluttered and draw the viewer's attention away from where it needs to be focused.

High depth of field makes better sense for landscape shots, crowd pictures, and similar photography where everything in the picture contributes to the whole. But that's only scratching the surface of the uses of aperture in photography.

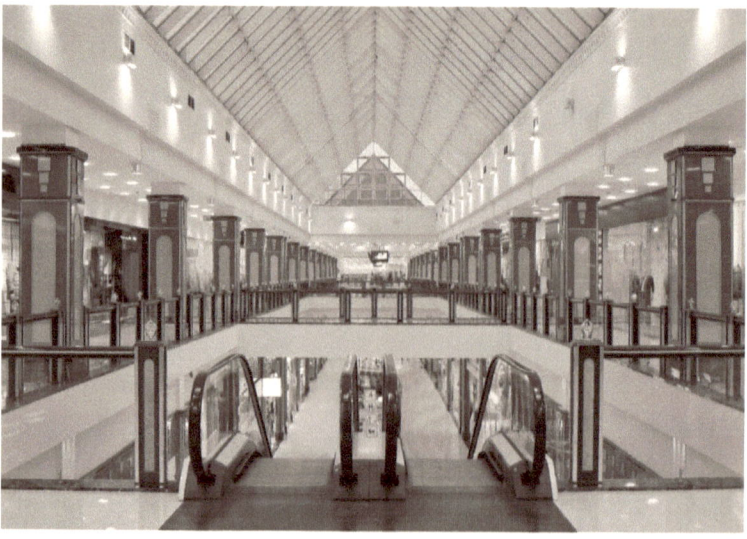

In this photo, note that both the nearby and more distant objects are in sharp focus. This is an example of high depth of field.

You should also remember that very small apertures, while they maximize depth of field, also lower the sharp focus of the entire picture, due to the increased effect of light distortion when only a tiny amount of light is allowed into the camera.

F-Stop

The aperture of a camera is like the iris of your eye, but unlike your own iris, the camera's aperture has limited discrete settings rather than an unlimited range. The measure of the aperture's size is the f-stop.

Different lenses have different maximum apertures. The *focal length* of a lens is, technically, the distance in millimeters from the center plane of the lens to the sensor of the camera. The greater the focal length, the narrower the lens focus and the greater the potential magnification effect. Our own eyes have a focal length, measured from the center plane of the eye's lens to the retina, of about 43 mm. Lenses with a focal length of 35-70 mm are considered "normal" lenses because they mimic the eye's own focal length. Wide angle lenses have significantly shorter focal length, while telephoto lenses and zoom lenses on telephoto settings have significantly longer focal length.

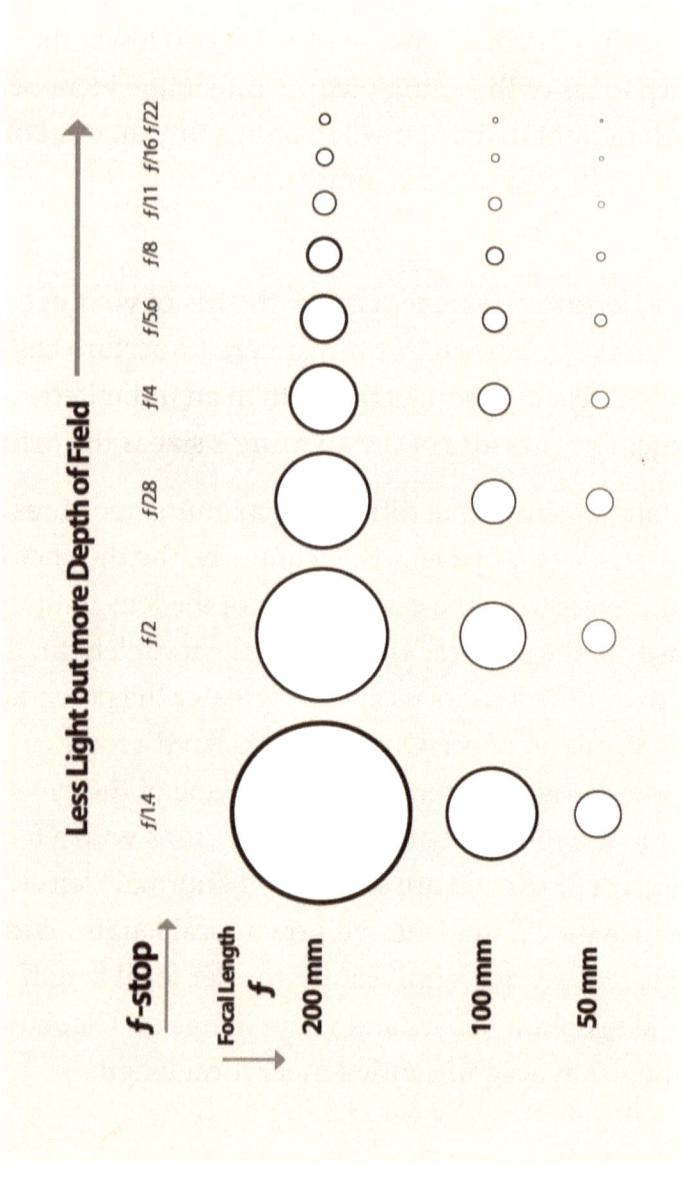

18

Each lens lists the focal length on its packaging and also the maximum f-stop, which looks like the minimum f-stop but isn't. Because of the technical nature of what's being measured – which actually isn't important for a photographer – the larger the f-stop, the narrower the aperture, so that f-1.4 is a wider aperture than f-8. Generally speaking, the smaller the aperture (that is, the higher the f-number), the wider the depth of field. However, it's also true that lenses with a shorter focal length have wider depth of field than those with a longer one, so a telephoto shot taken through a narrow aperture (high f-number) is likely to show lower depth of field than the same shot taken with a wide-angle lens.

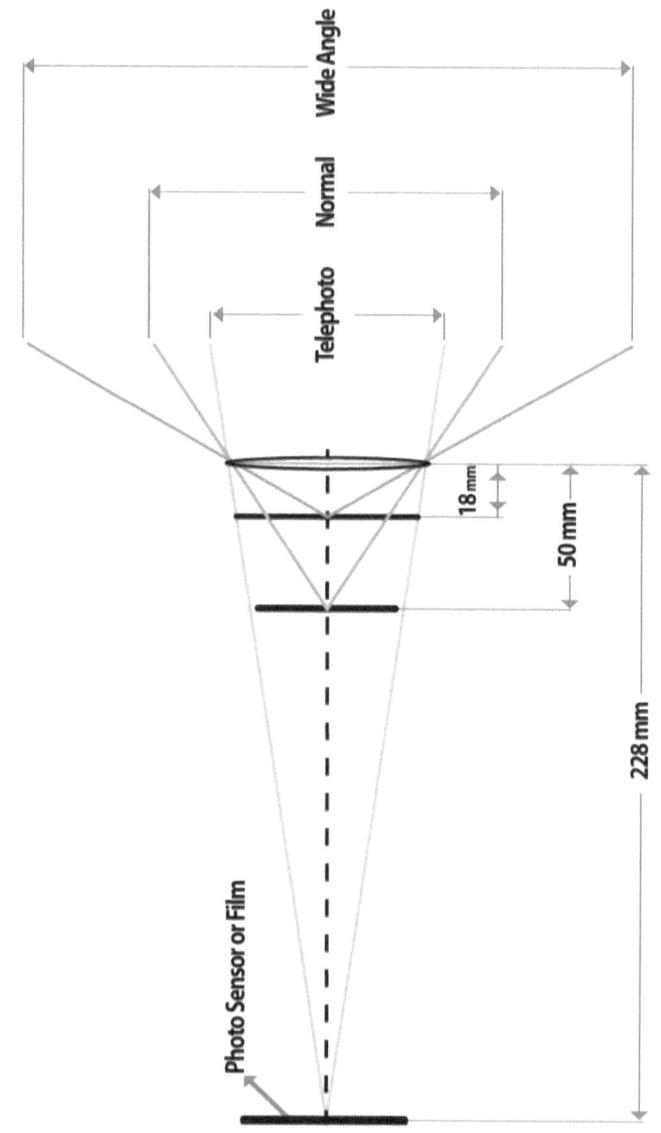

Here's another thing about f-stop measurements: they may not be in use for all that much longer. There's no particular reason why an aperture can't be set to any size, or why it has to be confined to particular sizes. The only reason why this became a photography convention is because of the relationship between aperture and shutter speed. With a narrower aperture, shutter speed needs to be set slower to compensate. Fixed f-stop variables were used with conventional cameras to allow accurate compensation using slower or faster shutter speeds. Digital cameras, though, allow for tighter control of shutter speed, which means that more variation in aperture becomes possible. For the present, however, f-stop remains the measure used for aperture in photography, and it's useful in describing how to set up photographic shots, so we'll use it in this book.

For practical purposes, all you really need to know is that f-stop is a measure of aperture that goes in reverse. If you set the aperture to a larger-number f-stop, you're narrowing it, allowing less light into the camera at any one time, increasing the depth of field, and requiring a slower shutter speed to compensate. If you set the aperture to a smaller-number f-stop, you're widening it, allowing more light into the camera at any one time, decreasing the depth of field, and requiring a faster shutter speed to compensate.

A reduction of aperture by one whole number setting (e.g., from f-2 to f-3) cuts the exposure of any given photograph in half. You can compensate for this reduction by halving the shutter speed. Thus, a picture shot at f-1.4 and shutter speed 1/60 has the same exposure as one shot at f-2.4 and shutter speed 1/30. Of course, this will produce a different effect, even though the exposure is the same.

You can also produce the same effect on exposure as stepping down the aperture by using a neutral gray filter, as described below. This cuts down on the light entering the camera without increasing depth of field.

Understanding Shutter Speed

Unlike the f-stop measurement for aperture, the measurement of shutter speed is relatively straightforward. Shutter speed is measured in fractions of a second. A shutter speed of 30, for example, means that the camera is exposed to light for 1/30 of a second.

Here's how the shutter works. Except when you're actually taking a picture, your camera is entirely dark on the inside. No light is allowed in, and the electronic sensors detect nothing. The shutter is a mechanical barrier to light that slides out of the way for a fraction of a second when you push the button to "take the picture," allowing light to pass through the lens, strike the sensor, and create a picture. The shutter then returns to position and the camera's interior returns to darkness.

What's described above is a mechanical shutter, which is found on all traditional film cameras and many digital cameras including the high-quality single-lens reflex cameras which probably include yours, if you have an interest in serious photography. Some digital cameras have an electronic shutter instead. An electronic shutter takes advantage of the fact that the sensor in a digital camera is electronic and its sensitivity to light can, with a design that incorporates this feature, be turned on and off. This creates the effect of a shutter without any mechanical shutter at all. That's sure to be the type of shutter in your cell phone camera, for example.

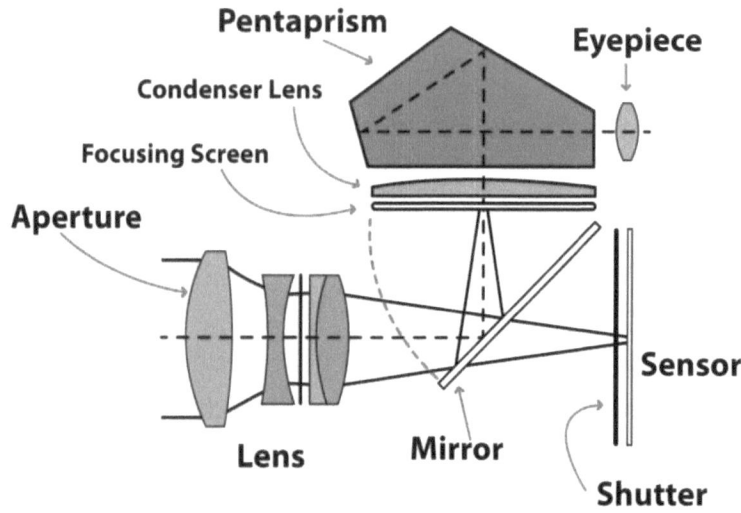

A digital single lens reflex camera's internal workings, including the shutter.

But in order to make use of this feature, the camera must incorporate what's called an "interline transfer sensor." This is a sensor where a part of each pixel is dedicated to storing the charge for that pixel, which makes the sensor that much less light-sensitive. This circuitry is necessary in order to provide the sensor with the on/off information, so that it is only operational when switched "on," and it reduces the effective quality of the camera. It does, however, greatly reduce the size of the camera, since the shutter mechanism is necessarily somewhat bulky. Where compactness is more important than the highest quality image, an electronic shutter with an interline transfer sensor is a good choice.

Higher-quality cameras use what are known as "full frame" sensors, where all of the circuitry is devoted to registering the light from the lens. Separate circuitry stores the image received by the sensor, which is always "on," and is activated by light itself. Full frame sensors are capable of producing a higher-quality image than interline transfer sensors, but require a mechanical shutter to take a picture, making cameras with that kind of sensor necessarily bulkier. Where the highest quality image is desired and compromising this value is unacceptable, a full frame sensor and a mechanical shutter are preferred. Obviously, that's the kind of camera that you want for photography as an art form.

Shutter Speed and Motion Capture

Shutter speed has a number of effects, but the most important one for creative photography is the ability (or inability) to capture motion.

Here's how that works. When you take a picture of something that's in motion, such as a person running or a car or an airplane or a bird in flight, the object moves during the time that the shutter is open. When the shutter first opens the object is at point A, and when it closes again the object is at point B. The faster the shutter speed, the less distance the object will be able to travel before the shutter closes again.

With a very fast shutter speed, most objects in motion won't have time to move very much during the exposure, and for all intents and purposes they will look as if they are standing still in the final image. With a slow shutter speed, the object will be able to move a considerable distance. To understand what happens as a result, remember that photography is all about light.

Let's say you're photographing a moving car using a slow shutter speed. You push the button and the shutter opens. Light reflects from the car at its starting position, enters the camera, and triggers a partial image. The shutter stays open. The car moves. Now, light reflects from the car at a new position, and creates another partial image when it strikes the sensor. The car moves again, light reflects from its new position, another partial image is created, and so on. Finally, the shutter closes, and the light reflected from the final position of the car before the shutter closes creates the final image of the car.

As a result, you have car images spread out over the trajectory of the car during the time when the shutter was open. The result is an image of a car at its final location, with a blurry streak behind it. This gives the visual impression of fast motion, but at the cost of less definition and detailed focus on the car itself.

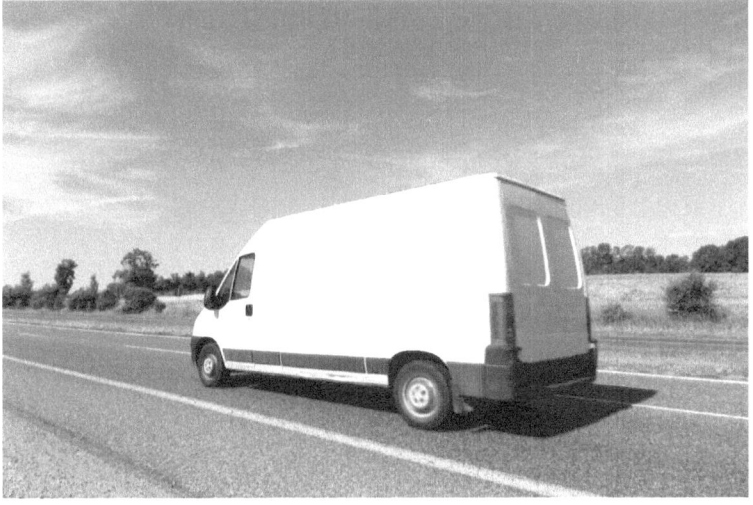

This van was photographed using a fast shutter speed. The motion of the vehicle is not visible.

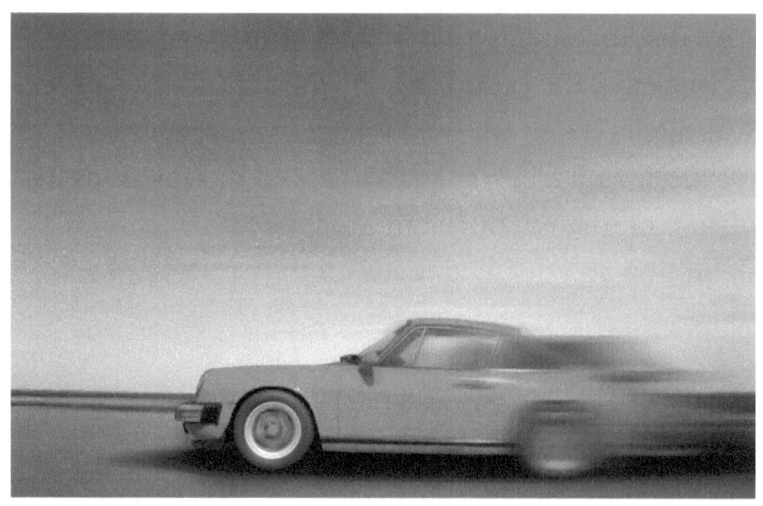

This sports car was photographed using a slower shutter speed. Note the motion blur.

Remember that aperture and shutter speed have a reciprocal relationship. Aperture controls how much light enters the camera at any given moment. Shutter speed controls how long the light is allowed to enter the camera. The combination of the two, along with the third point of the exposure triangle, ISO, determines how much light goes into creating the photographic image. Since shutter speed affects motion capture and aperture affects depth of field, these two controls can produce a wide variety of photographic effects.

Understanding ISO

The third point of the exposure triangle is the sensitivity of the photographic sensor, which is called ISO. ISO actually stands for International Standardization Organization. It's a professional body that issues standards for lots of different things, not just photography. Among photographers, though, when you use the term it's generally understood that you're referring to the light sensitivity originally of camera film, and today of electronic light sensors that take the place of film in digital photography.

ISO used to be called ASA. It's expressed as a number: ISO 100, 200, etc. The higher the number, the greater the sensitivity to light. With higher ISO settings, you can use faster shutter speeds and/or smaller apertures than you could with lower ones, in any given set of lighting conditions. The downside of this, though, is that higher ISO settings also produce grainier photographs with more visual "noise." So as with most things in photography, there's a trade-off. ISO 100 is considered a "normal" setting that produces nice, crisp, well-defined pictures with minimal noise. However, that doesn't mean that ISO 100 is the best choice for all circumstances. It's seldom a good choice for dim-light photography, as it will render a photo too dark without resorting to very slow shutter speeds or even timed exposure measured in seconds or minutes.

Remember that the bottom line when it comes to exposure is to let in the right amount of light for the effect you want. That involves using all three points of the exposure triangle. If you leave your exposure controls on full automatic, your camera will take a reading of the available light. It will set ISO, shutter speed, and aperture so as to expose your shot "properly." It will keep ISO as low as possible, and set shutter speed and aperture to create the "desired" exposure. The problem is that this may not be the exposure *you* desire, with the effects you're looking for.

The thing to remember about ISO is that the lower the setting, the less room you have to play with shutter speed and aperture to produce the effects you want. If you have a low ISO, you *must* have a certain range of aperture and shutter speed in order to produce the proper exposure. If there's plenty of light, you're shooting a stationary subject rather than a moving one, you're using a tripod so your own motion isn't a factor, and it's important to minimize grain in your image, then a low ISO setting is a good choice. If you're shooting in dark conditions without a tripod, or you're photographing a moving subject and don't want a lot of motion blur, or you are taking a panorama shot and want plenty of depth of field, then a higher ISO setting may be the way to go.

Reviewing the Exposure Triangle

The exposure triangle consists of three points: ISO (sensitivity of the photographic sensor), shutter speed (the amount of time the camera is exposed to light), and aperture (the amount of light that is let in at any moment). Each of these produces a trade off in terms of image quality or effects.

Low ISO produces a fine image without a lot of graininess or visual "noise." It also requires a relatively slow shutter speed and/or wide aperture compared to higher ISO settings to achieve good exposure. Higher ISO produces a grainier image, but allows a wider range of shutter speed and aperture settings.

Fast shutter speed captures motion well, without any motion blur, but requires either wider aperture or higher ISO, or both, to give you sufficient exposure. Slow shutter speed turns moving objects into a blurry streak in the image (which may or may not be the effect you want).

Wide aperture produces an image with low depth of field, while narrow aperture produces an image with greater depth of field. At the same time, narrow aperture reduces exposure, and so requires a slower shutter speed or higher ISO settings, or both, to achieve proper exposure.

Those are the elements and parameters of using exposure creatively in a nutshell.

Now let's go into the details and explore some of the things you can do with it.

About Light Metering

Your camera's light meter is an instrument that measures the intensity of light. However, it doesn't simply scan the entire area in view and measure all of the light reflecting from it. That's not how the technology works (although it would be nice to have that ability). Instead, it measures the light in one small portion of the field of view. Usually (although not always), the light meter takes multiple readings from various parts of the field of view and creates a recommended exposure setting from these samplings using an averaging algorithm. The light meter can be set to detect the light in several different ways.

Evaluative metering examines the light in multiple regions of the image area and selects or suggests exposure settings based on the average light intensity in all of these regions. This is also known as the "averaging" method.

Partial metering examines the light in the center of the image and a small area around it (less than 10 percent).

Spot metering is a more tightly-focused version of partial metering that measures the light in the center of the image and about 3.5% of the field around it.

Center weighted metering is similar to evaluative metering, but placing more emphasis on the center of the picture.

Most cameras allow you to select what type of light metering to use. You can also resort to a hand-held light meter that has more precise controls than are available in most built-in light meters. Evaluative metering is the kind most widely used, and is likely to be the best choice for most of your photographic efforts. It's also probably your default setting. However, depending on the type of shot you're taking, it may not be the best choice in every instance. If you're taking a picture where the center of focus outweighs everything else in importance, then it might make more sense to use one of the other methods. It can also give you a dramatically wrong result if you are taking a picture with high contrasts between light and dark areas. (See below regarding high dynamic contrast.)

Light metering, regardless of which method you use, informs your camera's automatic exposure settings, or you can use it to inform your own manual choices. Or a mix of both.

Histograms

On most cameras and all hand-held light meters, "histogram" appears as a menu option. A histogram is a graphic display of the light intensity ranges across the field of view. Rather than going by physical area, the histogram graphs the exposure based on shades and tones, from black at the far left to white at the far right. The higher the graph line at any point of the histogram, the more intensity of light in that shade. A histogram can show you whether your field of view is weighted towards the dark or light end of the spectrum, which can throw off your light metering.

The diagram is a specialized tool and, although useful in some circumstances, not essential to good creative photography or to handling exposure.

Exposure Compensation

Light meters are reliable under most circumstances, but there are some images that can throw it off and require you (or your camera's automatic settings) to compensate a bit. For example, suppose you are taking a picture of a lit-up city at night from a distance. Most of the picture area will be dark, and if you use that light metering result to set your exposure variables, you'll end up with overexposure on the part of the picture that you're interested in. You'll see an image of washed out glare rather than discretely sharp city lights. In a situation like that, it's necessary to do one of three things, compared to the settings recommended on the basis of the light metering: reduce the aperture, reduce the ISO, or increase the shutter speed. By doing that, you'll leave the area surrounding the city quite dark, but show the main point of the picture the way you want it to.

What this means is that the light meter should be treated as a guide, not a dictator. It usually gives you good information, but there are exceptions when you want to go against what it's telling you to do in one direction or the other.

Using the Camera's Light Meter

Your camera comes with a built-in light meter. To use the meter and obtain recommended settings for aperture and shutter speed, in most cameras, hold the shutter button down halfway. Looking through the viewfinder or at the display screen, you will see indicators for recommended settings. If your camera is set on full automatic exposure, these will be applied automatically. If you leave one or more settings on manual control, you will see an indicator of recommended settings and then be able to apply them before taking the picture by pushing the shutter button down fully.

Using a Hand-Held Light Meter

A hand-held, separate light meter is usually more precise than a camera-mounted light meter. It allows you to focus the metric area more tightly, down to 0.05% of the composition area, compared to a camera's spot meter mode which measures 3 to 5 percent of the composition area. A hand-held light meter can also be set to measure either of two modes.

Reflected Mode measures the light reflected from the scene. Point the meter to a middle-toned area of the composition and press the control to take a reading. Your light meter will recommend a combination of aperture and shutter speed for correct exposure. On most models, you can adjust one of these values and the meter will recommend a value for the other, adjusted to compensate for your choice.

Incident Mode is not available with a camera's light meter. With this mode selected, hold the meter directly in the path of the light source, whether it's sunlight or artificial light. Rather than measuring the light reflecting from the subject, your light meter in incident mode measures the light falling on the meter itself from the light source.

Either mode of measurement allows you to register the light more precisely and accurately than is possible with a camera's light meter. The downside is that the aperture and shutter speed must always be set manually, so that it takes longer to take the picture when using a separate light meter. For many photographic purposes, especially if you need to take a shot quickly, the camera's built in meter is adequate and convenient. Despite this, the increased accuracy, precision, and versatility of a separate meter makes it a worthwhile investment for anyone serious about photography as an art form.

While your camera's light meter is perfectly fine for most purposes, some types of photography benefit from using a hand-held exposure meter. That's especially so when you're taking a picture in complicated lighting conditions with lots of highlights and shadows.

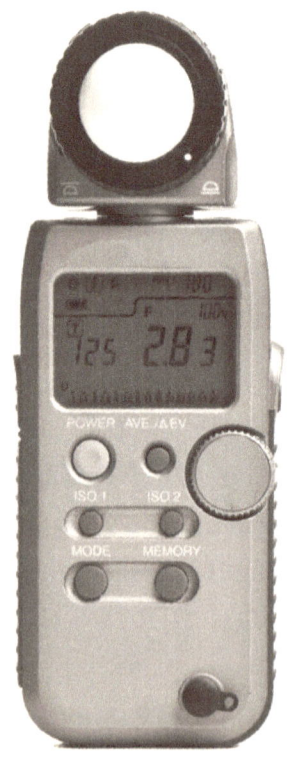

Hand-held exposure meter.

Light metering is a great tool, but like all tools it has its limitations and its flaws. Light meters make mistakes, mainly because they take measurements of light in only part of the picture and extrapolate from these measurements to an impression of the overall exposure needed to produce a good picture. That extrapolation can go seriously wrong if the light in a particular field of view is distorted by something.

Light metering methods usually work quite well when reflected light alone is involved, without the generation of light by part of the objects in view, and where extreme contrasts of light and shade are not present that can cause the meter to recommend or create over- or underexposure by taking samples of the wrong parts of the picture. Where objects in a field of view create their own light – city lights, car headlights, or in some cases stars or the moon – this can also throw off the light meter.

The brighter areas of a photo are called highlights. The darker areas are called shadows. Where the contrast between highlights and shadows isn't too great, or when there aren't too many of them, the light meter's averaging functions do a pretty good job. When the exposure is high enough to leave details in the highlights washed out, this is known as "highlight clipping." When the exposure is low enough to leave the shadows darkened and without much visible detail, this is known as "shadow clipping." Either of these is usually (although not always) a problem in photography. When you can see details with your eye that are important in the picture, but they don't show up in the photograph, then there's a problem with the exposure. A view area with a lot of contrast between the lightest and darkest areas is said to have "high dynamic contrast" and this presents some challenges when it comes to metering light.

There are several tricks using the light meter and the camera's auto-exposure devices to counteract these tendencies.

High Dynamic Contrast

High dynamic contrast (HDC) is a situation where extremes of bright and dark areas appear in a picture. A good example of this is an outdoor landscape picture including a bright sky and areas that are deeply in the shade. The problem here is that no single exposure setting will capture everything the way you want it to be seen. You can set your exposure to get the sky right, but then the shadowy areas will be dim and dark and effectively invisible. (The bright areas are known as highlights and the dark ones as shadow. Where they are effectively removed from the picture, this effect is known as highlight clipping or shadow clipping.) To capture this image correctly, it's usually necessary to take more than one photo and combine them using graphics software. Another approach is to use a polarizing filter to remove reflected glare, which can bring the highlights into proper exposure range.

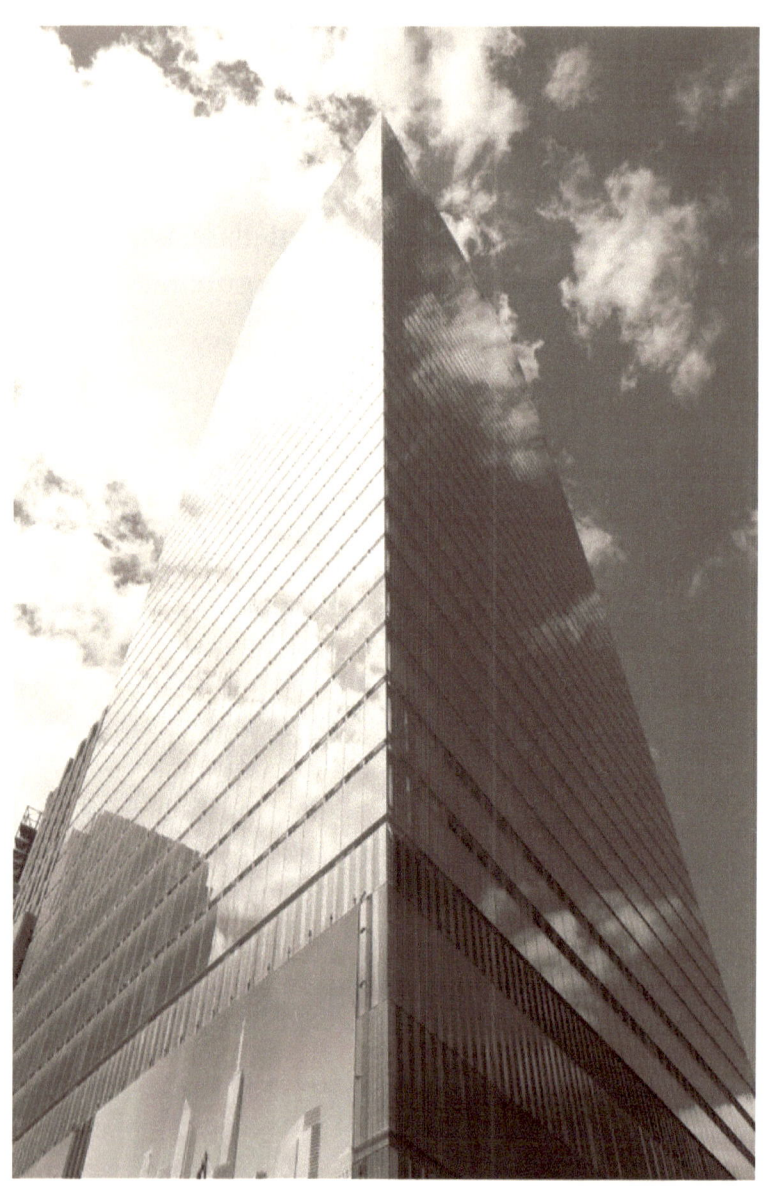

High dynamic contrast. The sunlit side of the building with its high reflectivity, and the bright sky and clouds, are

highlights, while the shadowed side with its deep shade is a
shadow. A difficult image to expose properly.

Exposure Bracketing

This is a method a lot of photographers use when
confronted with high dynamic contrast and exposure
difficulties. It involves taking three pictures in rapid
succession and combining them on the back end
using graphic software. The three photographs are:
one at normal exposure, one darker than normal, and
one lighter than normal. It's very important to use a
tripod and a remote shutter release when using
exposure bracketing, because otherwise camera
movements (even very slight ones) can distort the
alignment between the photos, making it difficult to
impossible to combine them on the back end.

You can use the same method without resorting to
graphic software just to be sure of the exposure when
the contrast is enough to make things uncertain. (For
that purpose, a tripod and remote shutter release
aren't as crucial, since you aren't going to be
combining the images.) For this, you simply pick
which exposure looks the best, and use that as a guide
when setting exposure of further images. One of the
great things about digital photography, remember, is
that you can check results immediately, while with
film photography you have to wait until the image is

developed, resulting in more wasted time. This makes experimentation a lot easier than it used to be.

When you do combine the images, the result is called a composite and it's produced not by your camera but by a graphic software program such as Adobe Photoshop. Further tweaking of the images can produce results such as in the image below. This can sometimes be the only good way to create photographs of high dynamic range scenes that display all elements of the picture clearly in a single image. An exposure that gets the highlights right leaves the darker areas invisible, and one that brings the shadows into view leaves the highlights a white blur. Only the composite shows both clearly.

Some problems can arise when taking exposure bracketing shots. One involves windy days with vegetation in the picture's foreground. Wind causes any vegetation, especially trees or tall grasses, to move. This won't create a motion blur as it would with long exposure, since each shot is likely to use a fairly fast shutter speed, but there may be visible changes in position between the shots. If possible, it's best to frame the picture to leave such vegetation out of the shot, unless there's little wind. The same rule applies to any objects in motion in the picture, such as cars or moving animals or people.

A variation on exposure bracketing is to take several shots, each of them deliberately exposed to render a portion of the scene perfectly. For example, in a landscape image with a very bright sky and a darker foreground, you could use spot metering or center weighted metering to find the "right" exposure for each of these, and then (with the camera in a fixed position – write down the settings if needed rather than letting the camera set them automatically, or use a separate light meter for ideal results) take a shot with each exposure setting. The composite photo is then created using the layer masks in your graphic software program, with each of the photos comprising one layer. In each layer, mask over the wrongly-exposed areas, leaving only the desired area visible in the layer. Combining them into a single image gives a desirable picture.

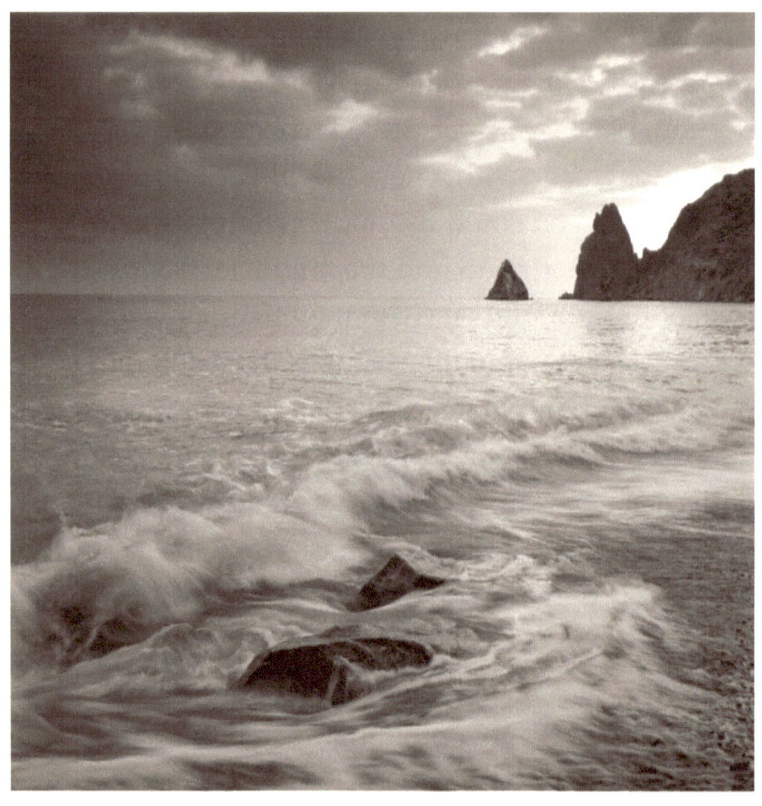

Composite photo taken using exposure bracketing techniques.

The photographer's art sometimes involves as much outside the act of taking a picture as inside it. That's even truer in the age of digital photography than with analog photography, although with that as well, a lot has always been done in the darkroom and the process of developing the image.

For many purposes, including exposure bracketing, it's a good idea to invest in and use a separate, hand-held light meter rather than relying just on your camera's built-in meter. When taking a series of exposure bracketed shots, you want to leave your camera in one position on a tripod, which means you can't focus it on separate parts of the picture to obtain light meter results. A hand held light meter fixes this problem. You will, of course, have to manually set the aperture in accordance with the light meter results. (For this kind of picture, it's best to keep a fixed and fast shutter speed, and vary the exposure using the aperture.)

Light metering can be simple or it can be extremely complex. Remember that photography is, in the end, all about light, and so the more you know about the light conditions before shooting the picture, the less in the way of trial and error will be needed. Of course, trial and error is much easier and cheaper with digital photography than when using film, so don't hesitate to experiment.

Manual and Automatic Exposure

The three points of the exposure triangle, ISO, shutter speed, and aperture, can all be set automatically by your camera using information from your light meter, or you can set one or two of them, or all three, manually. The highest degree of control obviously comes from setting all three of them manually. Depending on what you're doing, that may or may not be the right approach. In most cases, actually, it isn't.

What is "Proper" Exposure?

"Proper" exposure is what will allow all of the objects framed in the picture to be seen with the desired clarity. That's a little unclear in itself, but it can't be helped; "proper" exposure is the exposure that you want to achieve the effect that you desire.

However, your camera's light meter and automatic settings have a built-in idea of what "proper" exposure consists of, and for ordinary snapshots and other not-especially-creative photographic purposes, it's usually right. When lighting is dim, your camera will either lower shutter speed, increase aperture, or raise ISO, or some combination of these, compared to what it will do when you are shooting in bright light. If you let in too much light, your picture will have a washed-out appearance, while if you let in too little, it will be dark and dim. The light meter and the automatic settings work to avoid this.

Av Mode

In this partial-automatic mode, you control the aperture setting and let your camera set the shutter speed. This is a good choice when depth of field is the crucial element in your picture. When you set your aperture wide for low depth of field, your camera will automatically use a faster shutter speed than it will when you set your aperture narrow for high depth of field.

Tv Mode

This mode of operation is the exact opposite of Av mode. You control the shutter speed, and the camera automatically sets the aperture. This is the right approach when motion capture is all important, or when you are trying for a special shutter-speed effect such as those we'll discuss in a bit. Depending on what shutter speed you use, you may end up with a picture that has very high or low depth of field, as the camera adjusts the aperture to compensate.

Dual- and Full-Manual Mode

You can also choose to set both aperture and shutter speed manually, or to set all three points of the exposure triangle manually. Whatever your choice, there's a trade-off between control and ease of use. It's obviously easiest to let the camera set everything for you, but that restricts your control of the resulting image drastically. Setting everything manually gives you the ability to fine-tune the image most exactly, but you may end up spending a lot of time and effort adjusting settings that don't matter for the image you're trying to take.

Understanding the effects of ISO, shutter speed, and aperture on various aspects of the image (graininess, motion capture, depth of field) lets you determine which ones you need to control manually, and which ones you can allow the camera to set automatically, for any particular photograph. It's actually rather rare that you would benefit from manually setting all three of these. The one you'll most commonly want to leave on automatic is ISO. Whether you want to let the camera set shutter speed or aperture, or neither, depends on what type of picture you're taking.

As we move into more detailed discussion of artistic use of exposure in photography with specific examples, we'll mostly be focusing on either shutter speed or aperture, and in most cases it's acceptable and convenient to let the camera set the other.

Shutter Speed Effects

Remember that shutter speed affects motion capture. A fast shutter speed visually stops the motion of an object and freezes everything at a single moment, while a slower shutter speed leaves the moving object appearing as a blur. But that's only the beginning of the range of effects that are possible using shutter speed. Here are some of the more interesting effects that play off of this factor. Of the three points of the exposure triangle, shutter speed is the most versatile in the range of effects it can create.

Photographing Lightning

Lightning is so fast that "lightning fast" is a cliché. So you'd think that in photographing lightning, you'd want to use a really fast shutter speed, right? But you'd be wrong.

Here's the thing about lightning. It's actually *too* fast to manually capture the shot with a fast shutter speed. You see the lightning, and by the time you can bring your camera to bear on it, it's gone. At the same time, lightning is only visible very briefly. It flashes instantly, and then it disappears. It's less like a fast-moving object than one that appears and disappears without actually moving at all.

To photograph lightning, what you want is a very *slow* shutter speed and a narrow aperture and low ISO – and a tripod for stability. During the storm, frame a shot with a nice view of where lightning is about to appear. Use a shutter speed measured in whole seconds, as much as 30 seconds. Then repeatedly take pictures of the empty sky, over and over again. During one or more of those 30-second periods when the shutter is open, lightning will flash. The shutter is open for some time before and after the lightning flash, but the lightning itself appears only briefly, so it will appear with crisp definition in your image. You may need to do this quite a few times before you obtain the shot you want.

Recommended Equipment

For slow exposure photography, a tripod is a must. Otherwise, your own motion will distort the picture.

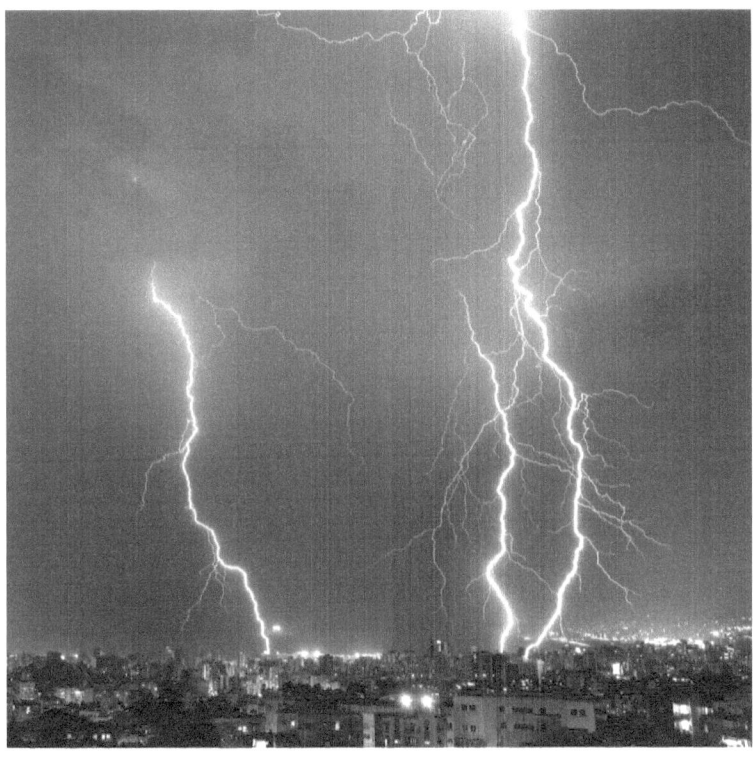

Photograph of lightning using slow shutter speed and low aperture.

An Empty City Street

Here's an interesting trick that uses very long exposure times (very slow shutter speed) and a low aperture. In this case, we're talking about a very long exposure, several minutes in total. The shot is taken using a tripod (long exposure shots should always employ a tripod for stability) of a city street at night. The method allows you to create an image with all of the architectural character and lighting quality on the street, but without any people. Pedestrians and vehicular traffic alike simply disappear from the image.

How does this work? With a low aperture, a long exposure is required to register an image of anything on the picture. Moving objects such as pedestrians and cars won't be in view for long enough for this to happen, while the objects that remain stationary, such as the street itself, the buildings, parked vehicles, and lighting and décor, will show up. The visual result will be an empty street.

You can do the same thing in daylight using a very dark neutral gray filter. Like other filters, this is something that screws onto the front of your camera lens. A neutral gray filter has no effect on the color of your image. It reduces the total amount of light coming into your lens, effectively darkening the image. This allows you to use the method above, with a long exposure, in daylight, which would ordinarily be prohibitive because it would overexpose the shot. Neutral gray filters are rated as multipliers: 2X, 3X, etc. The filter reduces the light coming into the camera by the amount of the multiplier (e.g., a 2X filter cuts the light by half, a 3X filter divides it by three, etc.). Remember that a full f-stop number increase cuts the light in half, too? This means that a 2X filter works the same as reducing the aperture by one f-number, and so on.

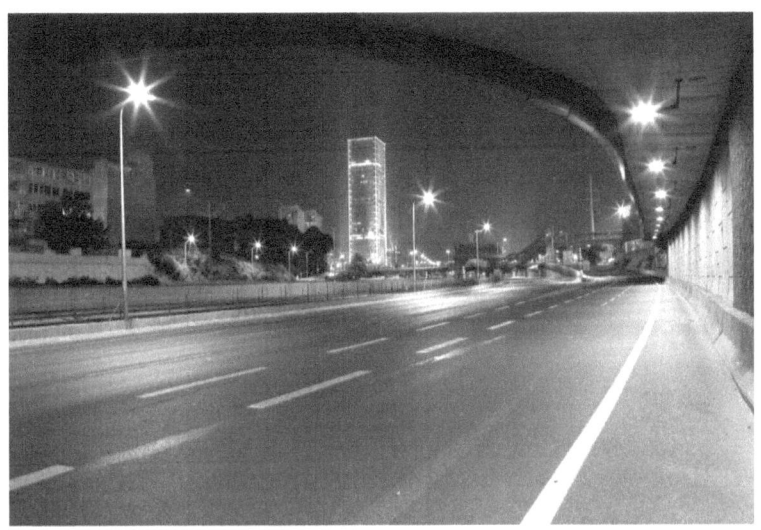

Emptied street shot with slow shutter speed and low aperture. Note the streetlight starburst effect as well as the vanished cars.

Panning

Another technique related to shutter speed is panning. When you hold the camera still and take a shot, unless you are using a very fast shutter speed, fast moving objects appear with motion streaks and are likely to be blurred. This is one way to create an impression of motion in your picture.

Panning, however, does exactly the opposite. Instead of holding the camera steady, you keep it focused on a moving object and move the camera so as to do this. Keeping the moving object in constant center focus while taking the picture produces an image where the moving object seems stationary, while everything else appears to be in motion. This is just the way you would see it if you were riding in a moving car, for example, or rather if you were riding along beside a moving car, or in a sidecar on a motorcycle, or something like that. The image is very different in detail, but creates much the same impression of speed, and leaves the object itself in clearer view.

Sometimes it's difficult to keep the object in focus when it's moving quickly and also difficult to do so without your own motion causing distortion. A tripod with rotation capability is sometimes used to stabilize the camera while taking panning shots.

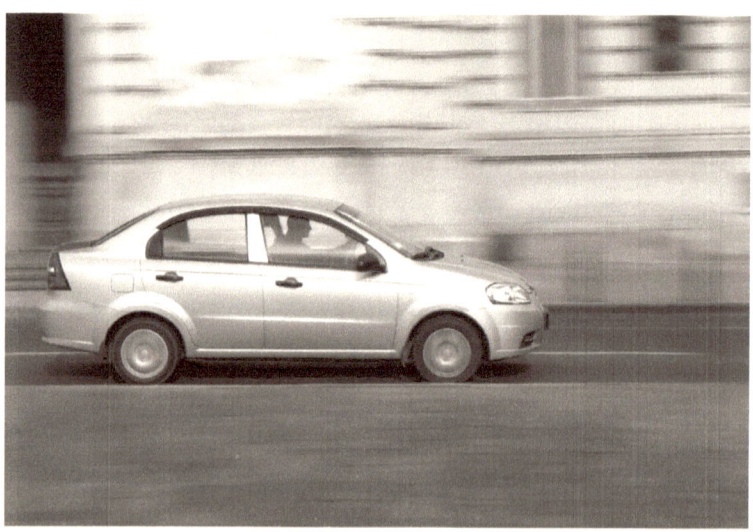

Panning: the moving car is in sharp focus while the background is blurred by motion.

When taking panning shots, the shutter speed shouldn't be set too fast or slow. Somewhere between 1/30 and 1/250 is the usual recommended range.

Light Painting

You can use a slow shutter speed (several seconds usually) to produce "light painting" pictures using a movable light source such as a sparkler or a flashlight. Hold the camera steady (use a tripod) and take the picture while the light source is in motion. A lot of interesting effects can be produced this way, with impressions of magical spells or super-powers, or other fantastic images. Some trial and error is likely to be necessary before you get the right exposure time for any given brightness of the light source.

Another example of light painting uses a laser pen in the dark to illuminate an object, such as a person's face. Set the camera on a tripod and use a long exposure, probably at least a minute. Make sure the laser pen is the only light source. "Draw" the contours of the face or other object using the laser pen while leaving the shutter open the whole time. Make sure your hands are outside the photo. The result is an eerie image and a cool effect. Try it.

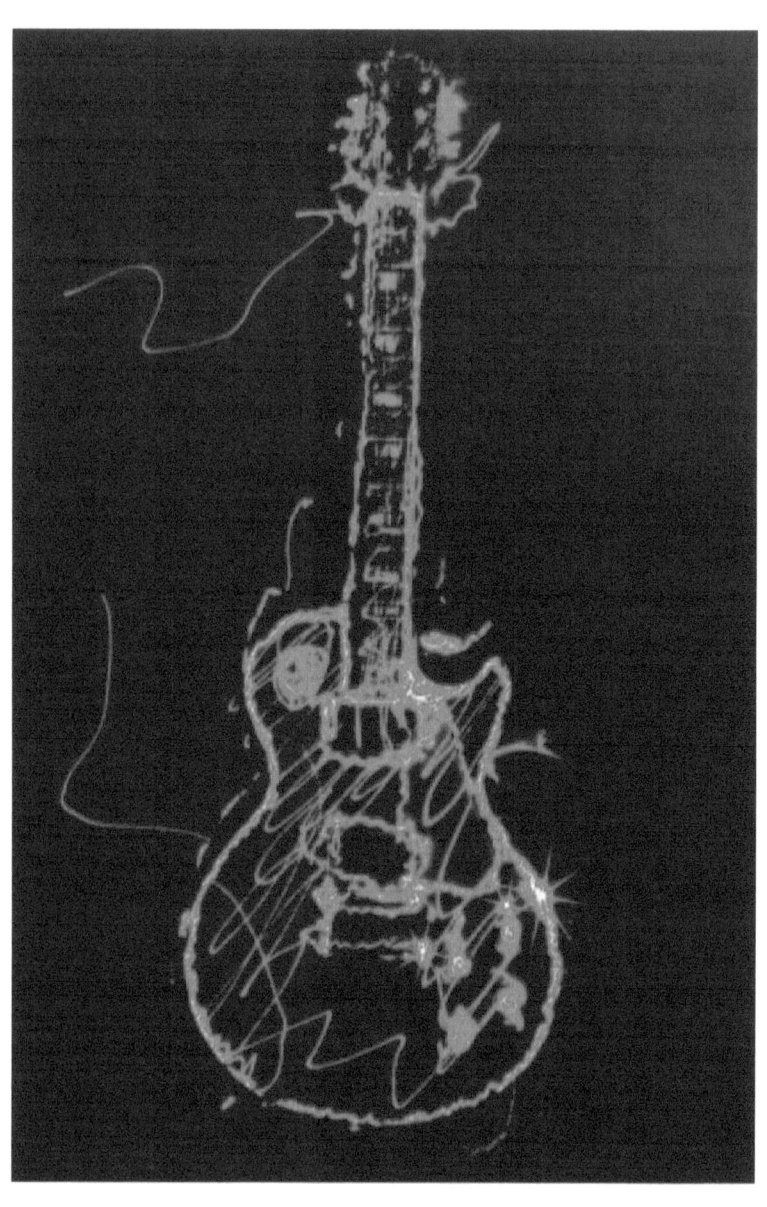

Laser "drawing" of a guitar using long exposure in the dark.

Whenever you use a slow shutter speed to produce an effect like this, it's important to step the aperture down from what your camera recommends at that shutter speed and ambient light.

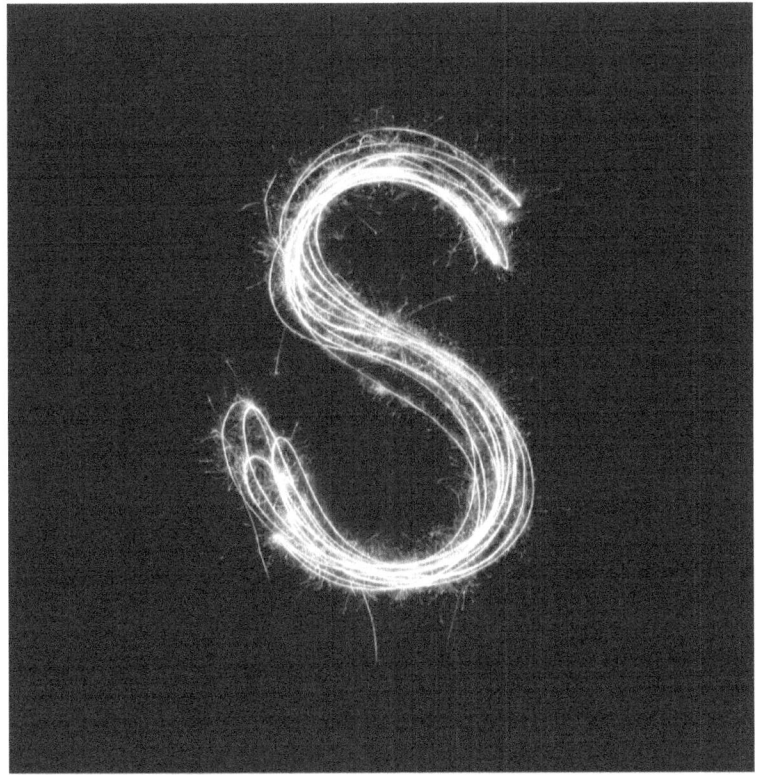

A "light painting" effect photo using timed exposure.

Traffic Patterns

A similar effect, and a type of light painting shot, involves patterns of traffic on a road, especially a highway. Take the shot at night when cars have their headlights on. Use a long exposure time, such as 30 seconds, and a stepped-down aperture. The result will show streaks of white light down one side of the highway and red light down the other. This can be particularly dramatic when used to shoot a complicated traffic pattern such as a clover-leaf intersection, or a busy intersection on city streets.

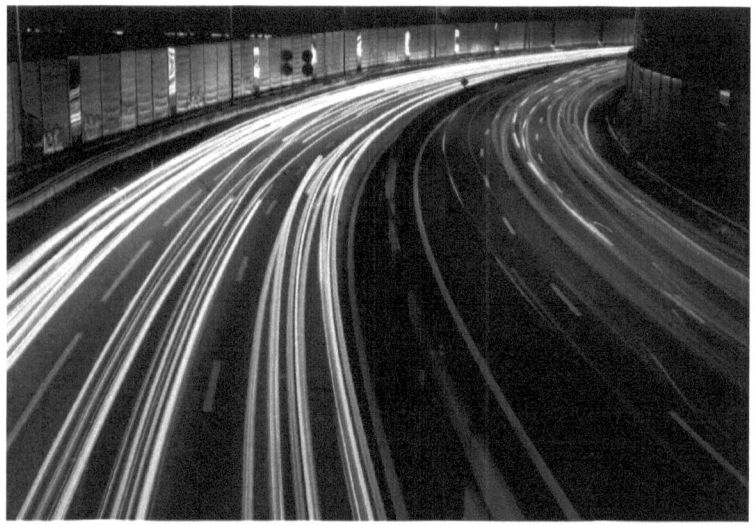

Timed exposure of busy highway at night.

Showing the Earth's Rotation

A similar effect using very long exposure – many minutes long – can produce an interesting effect at night that reflects the rotation of the planet. Pick a spot in the sky to focus the camera and let the shot run for 20 minutes or more. (Of course, you'll want to use a pretty low aperture for this. Also, you'll want to use a tripod, obviously.) As the Earth rotates and the stars appear to move through the sky, they'll form beautiful streaks of light in perfect circles around the camera's center of focus. You can achieve different effects with this method by having stationary framing objects in view, and by choosing to take the picture with or without the moon in sight.

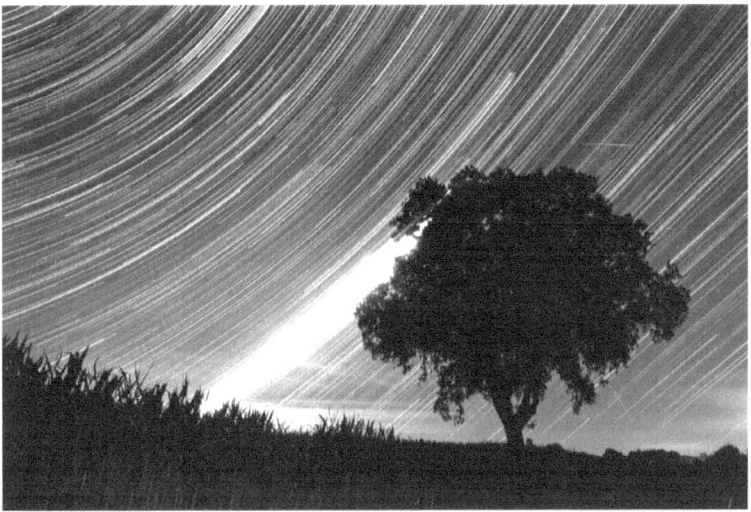

Long exposure photo showing light streaks from starlight, reflecting the Earth's rotation.

Motion Against Stillness

Long or timed exposure is also great for effects that don't involve light sources. A classic way to photograph a waterfall is to use a long exposure time. The rocky face of the waterfall doesn't move, so it's captured crisply, while the falling water gives an impression of motion and softness. An elegant image results.

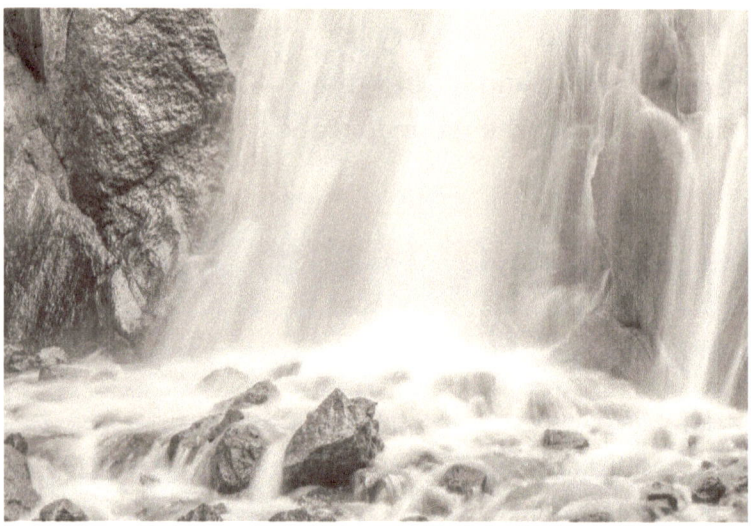

Waterfall captured using long exposure time.

The same method can give you a foggy image, an impression of soft motion in a fountain, and other similar images involving motion, especially of water or mist.

And of course, timed exposure is great for what it was originally designed for: capturing scenes in very dim light without using artificial lighting, high ISO, or wide apertures.

Freezing Action

Contrary to all of the above, if you want to freeze the action for moving objects, you need to use a fast shutter speed with a correspondingly higher aperture or, if you want to avoid low depth of field, higher ISO.

Usually a speed of 1/125 will freeze the motion of people and animals, but faster speeds may be necessary to capture the motion of a really fast animal such as a racehorse or a cheetah, or fast-moving vehicles.

One thing to bear in mind is that it's the *apparent* motion of the object that counts here, not its actual velocity relative to the Earth as a frame of reference. A car driving 65 miles per hour down the freeway, 20 feet away from you, has a higher apparent motion than an airplane that's moving much faster, but is further away. The closer an object is to you, the higher its apparent motion at any given speed. Also, your lens makes a difference. A telephoto lens which magnifies a distant object makes it appear "closer" than a normal lens, and this increases the apparent motion.

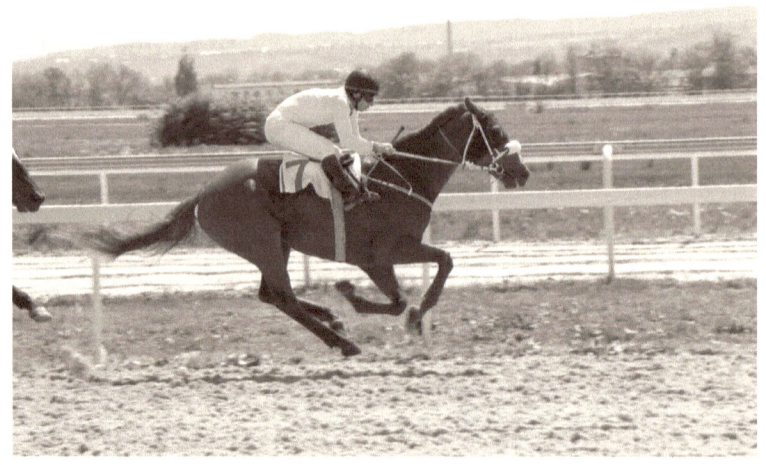

Photo of a galloping racehorse using very fast shutter speed to capture the moving horse and jockey in crisp focus.

It's not always desirable to completely freeze the action of a moving object. Using a very fast shutter speed, you can take a picture of a galloping racehorse with all four feet off the ground and clear to view. Perhaps this is the shot you want. In that case, go ahead and use that very fast shutter speed (probably 1/1000 would do the trick). However, a slightly slower shutter speed might show the horse's body clearly, but leave the legs streaked and blurred and give an impression of furious speed. That can be a nice shot, too. It all depends on what you're trying to do.

Recap of Shutter Speed

Shutter speed represents the amount of time that your camera is open and allows light in. The slower the shutter speed, the longer the exposure time. The longer the exposure time, of course, the greater the total exposure.

The main effect of shutter speed is on motion capture. A fast shutter speed lets you capture fast-moving objects without motion streaks. A slower shutter speed allows for motion blurring either of the moving object itself or, with panning, of everything else in the picture. In all cases, the inverse relationship between shutter speed and aperture needs to be kept in mind, with slower shutter speeds requiring a narrower aperture, while faster shutter speeds require a wider aperture, to achieve correct exposure. Also, bear in mind that with slow shutter speed, the motion of the camera may become a factor. Slow shutter speeds require use of a tripod to avoid camera vibration causing blurring of the photo.

Many interesting effects can be achieved with very slow shutter speeds, usually called timed exposure. These include light painting, the elimination of moving objects from a picture, and recording of motion patterns such as traffic or even the rotation of the Earth.

Effects Using Aperture

The range of effects that can be achieved by varying the aperture isn't as great as what can be done with shutter speeds, but it's an important part of creative photography nevertheless. As noted above, aperture mainly impacts the photograph in terms of depth of field. A wide aperture results in lower depth of field, while a narrow aperture results in greater depth of field. In addition, of course, a wider aperture results in more exposure, allowing (or requiring) a lower ISO or a faster shutter speed than a narrow aperture. The range of effects from aperture may be less impressive than those from shutter speed, but they are very important effects. That's why a lot of photographers recommend using the Av mode, where you manually control the aperture (and keep it a constant, reflecting the depth of field effects that you want in the picture), while letting the camera automatically set the shutter speed, for most purposes.

Of course, "most purposes" doesn't mean "all purposes." There is no one single mode that's appropriate for all photography. A lot of the art comes from creative use of all aspects of exposure.

There are several classic forms of artistic photography which use aperture to produce desired effects.

Depth of Field In Depth

We've mentioned above two of the factors affecting depth of field in a photograph. One of these is aperture, with a wider aperture producing a lower depth of field. Another is the focal length of the lens. Focal length, once again, is the distance from the center plane of the lens to the light sensor of the camera. A short focal length such as with a wide angle lens produces greater depth of field while a long focal length as with a macro, telephoto or zoom lens gives less depth of field.

There are two other factors affecting depth of field. One of these is subject distance. The "subject" is the part of the picture where you center the camera, and to which you adjust the focus. The further away the subject where you focus the camera, the greater the depth of field. With very close subjects, you will have low depth of field even with very narrow apertures.

The fourth factor is the distance between the subject of the picture and objects in the background. Background objects that are further away from the subject create an effect similar to low depth of field. (It isn't actually low depth of field, but simply the fact that the background objects are outside the depth of field focus range. The visual effect is the same, however.)

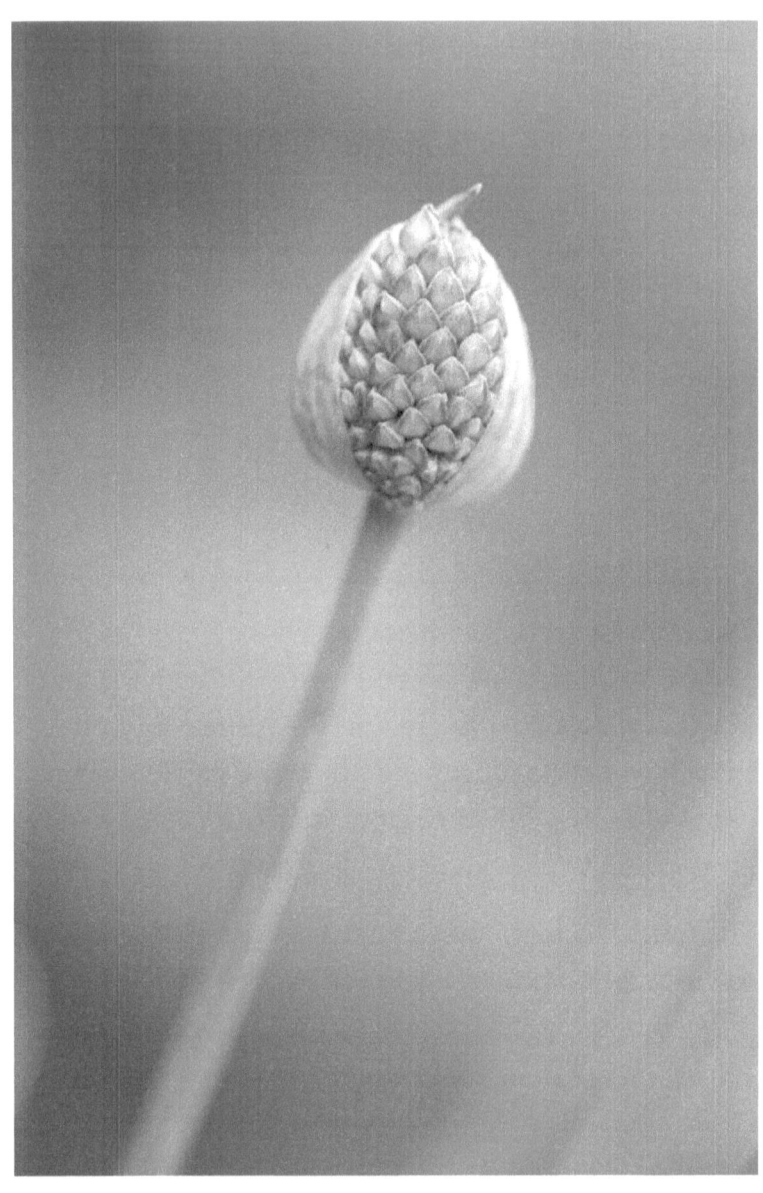

Close up of lavender bud using macro lens. The focal length produces low depth of field similar to a wide aperture.

It's important to keep all four of these factors in mind when setting aperture. As a general rule, wide aperture means low depth of field and narrow aperture means high depth of field, but because of focal length, subject distance, and subject to background distance, that's not universally true.

Portrait and Close-Up Photography

Portrait photography is usually done indoors under artificial lighting. Some portraiture, especially for commercial modeling purposes, is done outdoors. In both cases, almost always the main focus needs to be on the model or the portrait subject, rather than on the background. One classic way to do this is to use a wide aperture for a low depth of field. This gives the remainder of the picture a soft, somewhat out of focus look, and draws attention to the model. This blurring is known as "bokeh," from the Japanese word for blur.

There are exceptions, however. If you are composing a shot in which the model is engaged in an activity, then you will want the objects which comprise that activity to be clearly focused, as well. This may require a greater depth of field and so a narrower aperture than is used with classic portrait photography. As always, the other factors impacting depth of field should be kept in mind. With a short subject to background distance, for example, a good inclusive shot can be taken with a wide aperture.

Close-up photography using macro lenses also calls for a low depth of field. Some of this is actually provided by the macro lens itself, however, because of the long focal length of the macro lens. This makes use of aperture for the purpose unnecessary in many cases and allows using a narrower aperture with correspondingly greater freedom to set shutter speed and ISO to produce the desired image. The same is true of photography using a telephoto or zoom lens. Remember that depth of field is an inverse function of the focal length of the lens, as well as of aperture, subject distance, and subject to background distance.

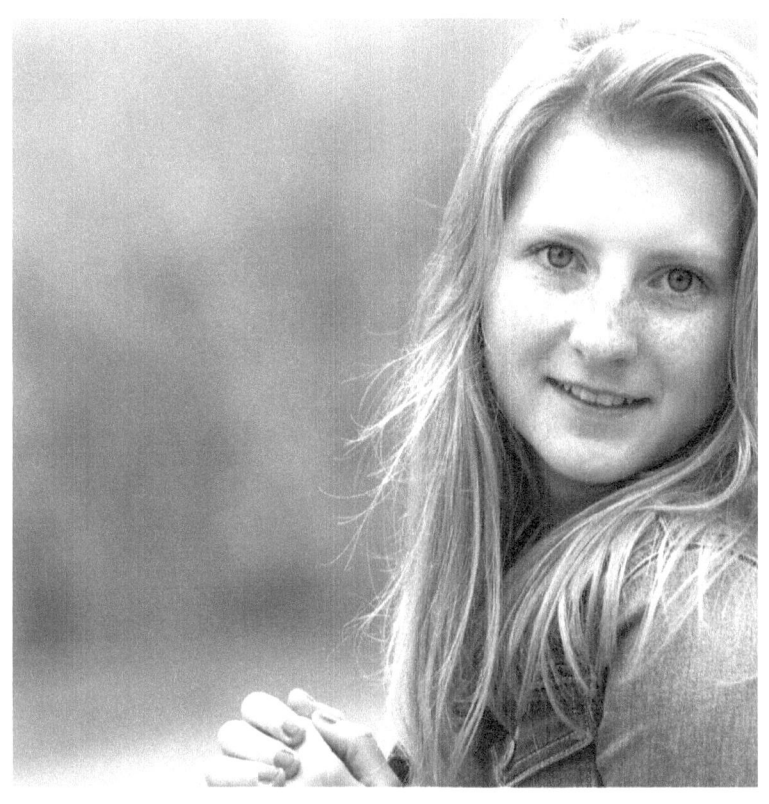

Outdoor portrait photo using wide aperture for low depth of field.

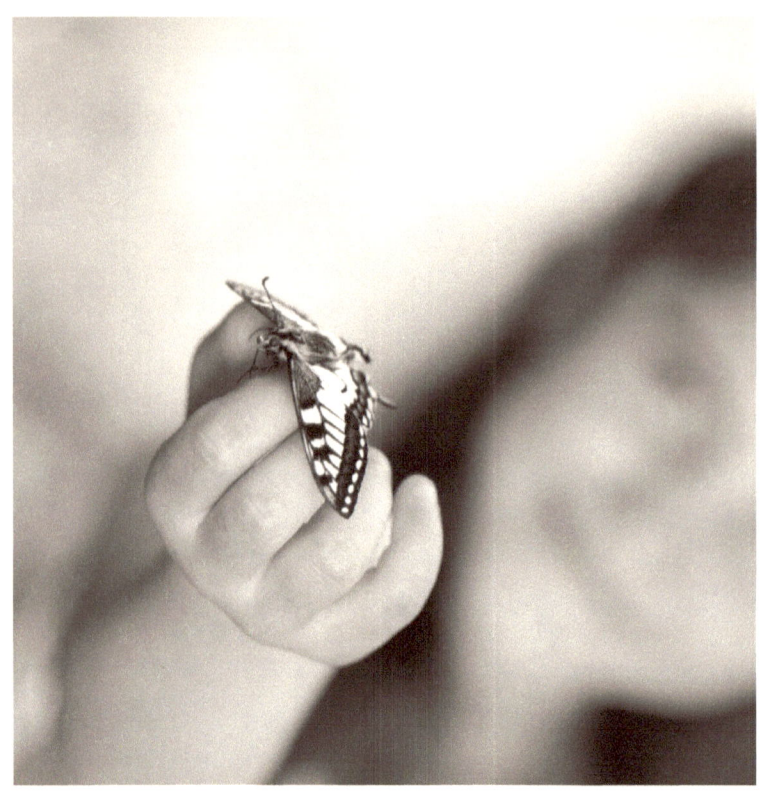

Close-up photo of a butterfly using a macro lens, showing low depth of field.

Panoramic and Landscape Photography

At the other end of the scale is panoramic and landscape photography, often employing a wide-angle lens. The wide-angle lens imparts a high depth of field in itself due to its short focal length, and using a narrow aperture increases the depth of field further. Usually in such images you want everything sharp and clear and don't want much in the way of bokeh. As always, however, there are exceptions. Bearing in mind the effect of aperture on depth of field lets you use it creatively to produce unusual images.

In all cases, remember the trade-off between aperture and shutter speed. A low aperture reduces exposure, which means you will need to slow down the shutter speed (or increase ISO) to compensate. It's a good idea to become familiar with the type of images your wide angle lens produces at various apertures.

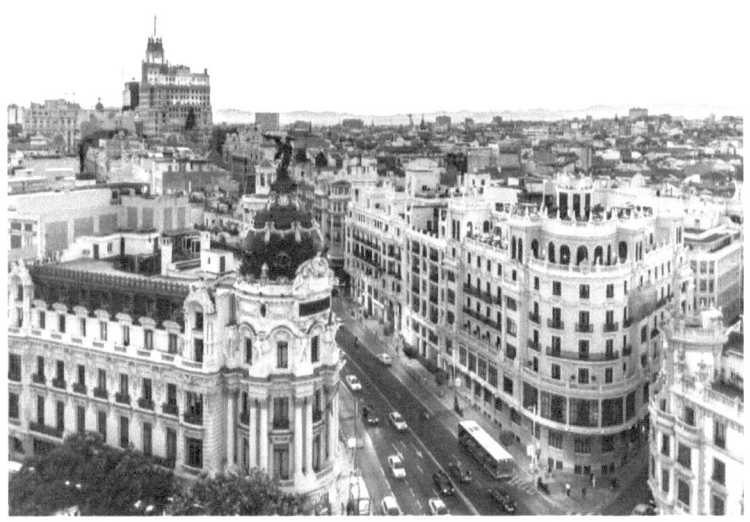

Panoramic photo of a downtown urban area (Madrid) using a narrow aperture and wide angle lens for high depth of field.

The Starburst Effect

When you photograph a light source directly, the image can produce a "starburst" image around the sun, moon, star, light bulb, or other source of radiance. The starburst is a result of diffraction. Diffraction (in this case) is a consequence of the light bending as it passes through the camera's small opening. What this means is that starburst effects are more pronounced when using a smaller aperture. A tight aperture like f/22 produces a very noticeable starburst effect, while a wide aperture such as f/4 can eliminate the starburst effect altogether.

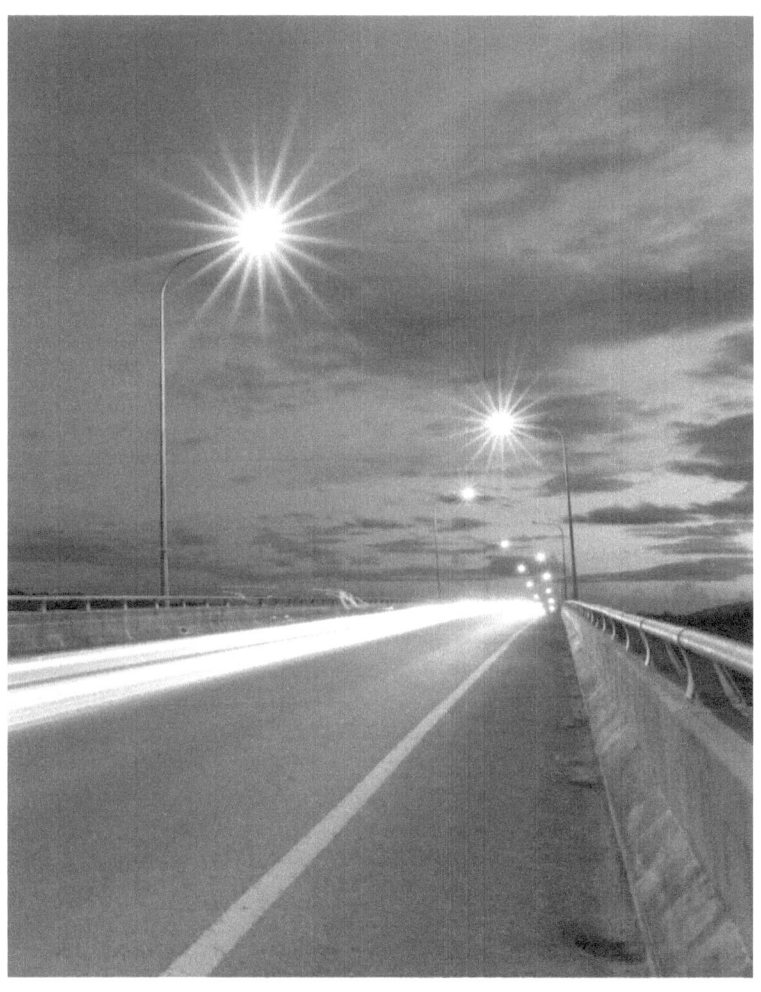

Streetlights at night, narrow aperture, showing the starburst effect.

Starbursts can add very dramatic effects to images with light sources contained in them, which may be what you're looking for or it may not, depending on the composition. Varying the aperture (and adjusting shutter speed or ISO accordingly) can change the image enormously.

Note that, unlike depth of field, the starburst effect is not produced by the focal length of the lens, subject distance, or subject to background distance. This is entirely a result of a narrow aperture, which of course also generates a high depth of field. That means that when you have a starburst effect you are more likely to have the light source in crisp focus even when it isn't your subject.

Using Filters

As noted above, a neutral gray filter can be used to cut down on light instead of lowering aperture when you want a low depth of field or want to use a slow shutter speed. Another filter that's useful in digital photography is the polarizing filter.

A polarizing filter can remove glare from reflected surfaces and is another way to eliminate highlight clipping from a picture with high dynamic contrast. A polarizing filter can remove the need for exposure bracketing and back-end photo processing to achieve such a picture, but produces a somewhat different effect.

Things to Know Before Buying

Photographic filters are easy to find, quite inexpensive, and of consistent quality. Just make sure that the filter is the right size to fit your lens and you're good to go.

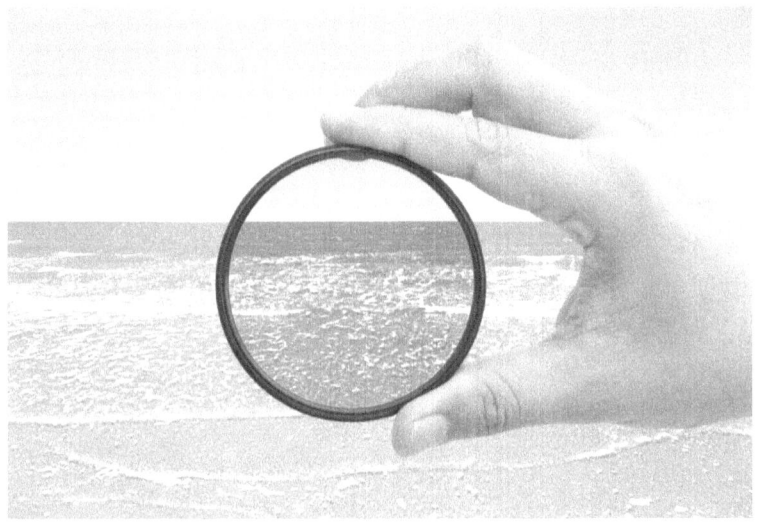

A picture taken both through and around a polarizing filter, showing the effect on highlights, shadows, and contrast.

Filters aren't as useful in their full range of possible effects for digital photography as for film photography, but those two types of filter – the neutral gray filter and the polarizing filter – are still important for some purposes.

Recap of Aperture

Aperture refers to the size of the hole through which light passes. It is measured inversely by f-stop, so that a larger number of f-stop such as f/22 represents a smaller aperture than a smaller f-number such as f/8. One whole f-number difference represents a doubling or halving of the amount of light coming in through the aperture.

The main effect of aperture on photography concerns depth of field, or how much of the photo is in focus. A low depth of field confines sharp focus to the main object of view and leaves most of the picture blurred. This results from a wide aperture. A higher depth of field has more of the picture in focus and results from a smaller aperture. Depth of field also varies inversely with the focal length of the lens and with subject to background distance, and directly with distance to the subject.

Aperture can produce a few other effects such as the starburst effect around light sources, which is more pronounced with a smaller aperture. Aperture has an inverse effect with shutter speed and ISO in terms of total exposure, so that reducing the aperture requires slowing the shutter speed and/or increasing the ISO to compensate.

ISO Settings

The third point of the exposure triangle produces the least in the way of interesting effects, but it's no less important because of two things. One is the increase in graininess or digital noise as ISO increases. The other is the limitation a lower ISO places on where you can set aperture or shutter speed and get a good exposure.

ISO settings follow a simple arithmetic scale. ISO 200 is twice as light-sensitive as ISO 100. The general rule is to keep ISO as low as you reasonably can, given the light conditions, but for some artistic shots a grainy photograph may actually be desired, making a higher ISO the right choice. A higher ISO is also desirable when shooting under dim light under conditions where, for one reason or another, you can't employ aperture or shutter speed to create the right exposure, and can't use a flash.

As a general guideline:

Use ISO 100-200 to take photographs in full daylight conditions. This gives you the maximum photographic quality, and the light is sufficient that there's no need for a higher ISO.

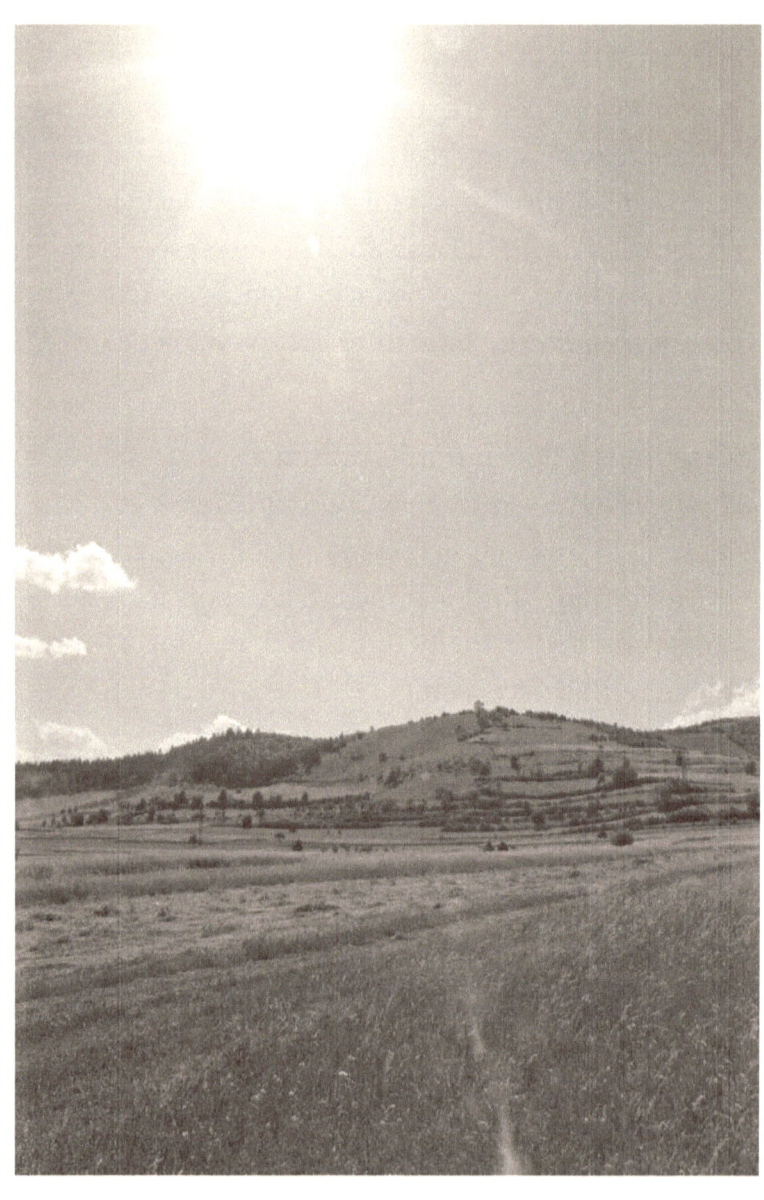

Outdoor panoramic photo shot at ISO 100

Use ISO 200-400 for slightly dimmer conditions, such as when your subject is in the shade, or indoors with bright artificial light.

Use ISO 400-800 when shooting indoors using a flash, in dimmer artificial light, or when taking an early morning or twilight outdoor shot.

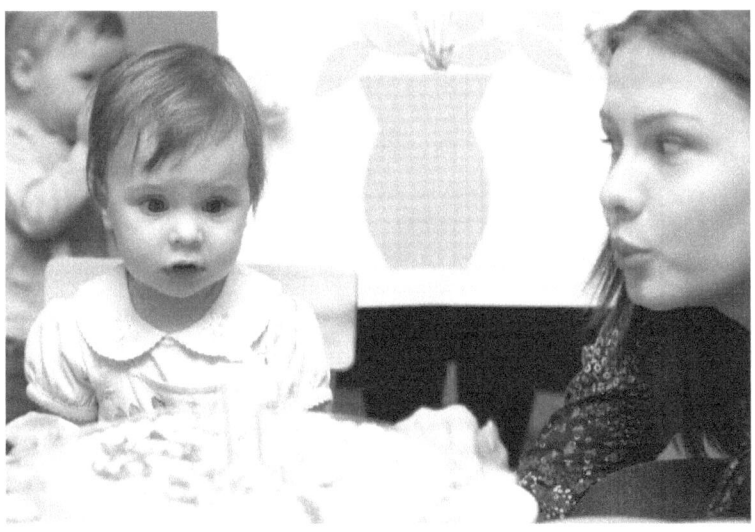

Indoor picture taken at ISO 400

ISO can be set as high as 3200 on most good digital cameras. Very high ISO settings like this produce unavoidable graininess, but have their uses. It is often necessary to use a high ISO setting when photographing indoor events such as a concert. The lighting is often quite low, and a flash isn't permitted. It's also not convenient to use a tripod, and even if you could, capturing the motion of performers, dancers, etc. is often important, so that a slow shutter speed isn't a good idea.

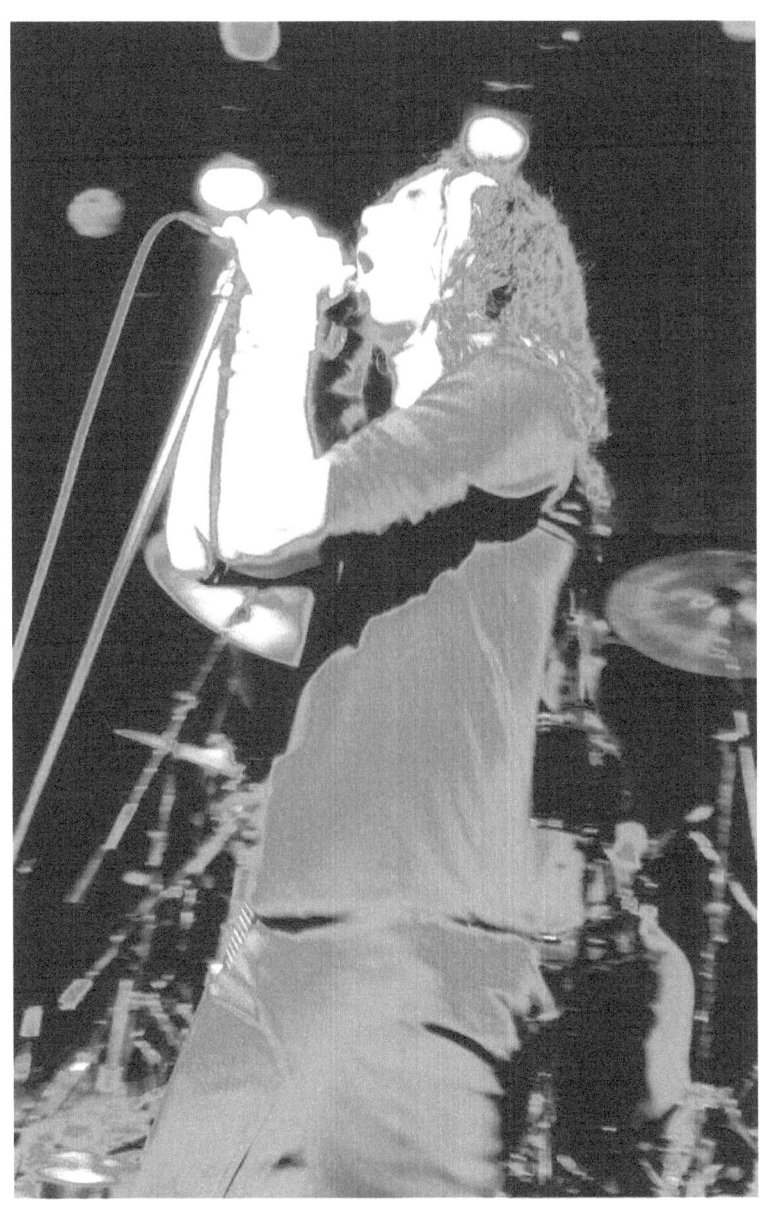

Deliberately grainy, abstract photograph taken at ISO 3200

As a general rule, the graininess that comes from using a high ISO is something to avoid. There are exceptions to almost every rule in photography, however, including this one. Sometimes creating a grainy, noisy image is exactly what you want, as in the example above.

Effect of ISO on Aperture and Shutter Speed

The three points of the exposure triangle, aperture, shutter speed, and ISO, work together to produce the desired exposure of a photograph. When one of the three is set low (fast shutter speed, narrow aperture, or low ISO), one or both of the other two must be set higher (slow shutter speed, wide aperture, or high ISO) to compensate, or the image will be underexposed. Except in very strong light conditions, it's generally not possible to set ISO low to minimize grain, shutter speed fast to capture motion, and aperture narrow to increase depth of field. Something has to "give" in order to let in enough light for long enough to take a clear picture.

The lower you set your ISO, the more you restrict your shutter speed and aperture options. However, the effect on the quality of the image from using a low ISO setting is positive enough that most photographers try to use the lowest ISO settings they can whenever light conditions permit.

In all cases, though, it's important to keep in mind that this trade-off exists. Those higher ISO settings exist for a reason: sometimes they're needed. If you don't use a higher ISO in dim light, then you must either increase aperture or reduce shutter speed or both.

Can you reduce the shutter speed? Or will doing that result in too much motion blur and other effects that you don't want? Can you widen the aperture? Or will doing that result in too low depth of field, when you are taking pictures where your focal length, subject distance, and subject to background distance mean you need a fairly high depth of field resulting from a narrower aperture?

If you can't use either shutter speed or aperture to provide the necessary exposure for some reason, then go ahead and raise the ISO setting. Doing this will increase the graininess of your photo, but sometimes that's a better option given the light conditions and other restrictions resulting from the type of photo you are taking.

Unless you're deliberately seeking a grainy quality to the photo, raising the ISO should be the last resort for increasing exposure, but that doesn't mean it should never be your choice.

Conclusion

Creative photography makes use of a number of factors in addition to those affecting exposure. The framing and composition of the picture, focus, and graphic image processing on the back end are just as important. As the overview presented in this book shows, however, exposure all by itself can produce a wide variety of photographic effects, encompassing motion capture, depth of field, diffraction, reflection, and other variables involving the processing of light.

There's a lot more detail on the subject that you can find online or in books about photography, but as with any art form, the best way to learn is to get a little guidance, some ideas, and some suggestions, and then practice. Take your camera out along with a few accessories – a hand-held light meter, a tripod, several lenses, perhaps a few neutral gray and polarizing filters – and start taking pictures.

A good exercise is to see for yourself what effects you can achieve by varying the points of the exposure triangle. See how pictures shot at 100 ISO differ from those shot at 400 ISO. Take a picture using a wide aperture and a fast shutter speed, and then the same picture using a narrow aperture and a slower shutter speed, and note the differences. See for yourself how highlights, shadows, and other areas of a picture emerge with different exposure settings. Deliberately under- and overexpose a picture – you might find that you like the effect, and learn that "correct" exposure is sometimes arbitrary.

The great thing about digital photography is that if you don't like the results of one approach to a picture, you can toss them in the trash with the touch of a button and try something else. There's no cost to experimentation except your time, so be lavish with it.

As you get practice, you'll find yourself looking at scenes with photography in mind, and a large part of that will encompass exposure. Should you use a fast shutter speed to capture that motion? Would a wide aperture zero in on just the element you want? What would this look like in a timed exposure? Would a polarizing filter be the best way to remove that glare? Along with these and other exposure-related questions, you'll ask yourself how the picture would best be framed and composed, what to include, what to leave out, what type of lens would capture the desired image best. You may find yourself looking at a single scene and imagining many different pictures from it, with different framing, cropping, focus elements, and exposure.

And that's what makes photography fun and an art form. Nature provides only the raw materials. Your mind uses your camera and other tools to create the picture from those raw materials, just as a painter uses pigments and canvas, or a sculptor uses marble or wood or clay.

Special Thanks

I would like to give special thanks to all the readers from around the globe who chose to share their kind and encouraging words with me.

Knowing even just one person found this book helpful means the world to me.

If you've benefited from this book at all, I would be honored to have you share your thoughts on it, so that others would get something valuable out of this book as well.

Your reviews are the fuel for my writing soul, and I'd be **<u>forever grateful</u>** to see *your* review, too.

Thank you all.

Check Out My Other Best-Selling Book:

- <u>DSLR Photography for Beginners</u>

www.ingramcontent.com/pod-product-compliance
Lightning Source LLC
Chambersburg PA
CBHW031923170526
45157CB00008B/3035